SCHOLASTIC

Great GLYPHS

All About Me

12 Skill-Building Activities That Motivate Kids to Collect, Display, and Use Data—and Connect to the NCTM Standards

by Patricia Daly and Teresa Cornell

NEW YORK • TORONTO • LONDON • AUCKLAND • SYDNEY
MEXICO CITY • NEW DELHI • HONG KONG • BUENOS AIRES

Teaching *Resources*

To my son Michael—The light of my life!
—P. D.

To Charlie,
You are my sunshine!
I love you, Mommy.
—T. C.

Edited by Immacula A. Rhodes
Cover design by Maria Lilja and Norma Ortiz
Interior design by Holly Grundon
Cover and interior illustrations by Maxie Chambliss

ISBN: 0-439-41431-8
Copyright © 2006 by Patricia Daly and Teresa Cornell
Published by Scholastic Inc.

1 2 3 4 5 6 7 8 9 10   40   14 13 12 11 10 09 08 07 06

Contents

Glyphs

Introduction

In its *Principles and Standards for School Mathematics* (released April 2000), the National Council of Teachers of Mathematics (NCTM) identified Data Analysis, Statistics, and Probability as one of five key content-area standards. This standard addresses the importance of having students:

- pose questions

- collect, organize, and represent data to answer questions

- interpret data using methods of exploratory data analysis

- develop and evaluate inferences, predictions, and arguments based on data

This and other standards are included in the grid on page 9 to show how they correlate to each glyph activity.

For grades 1 to 3, the NCTM objectives and standards can best be met by involving students in meaningful, motivating activities that give them opportunities to collect and represent data in a variety of ways. Creating glyphs, or pictorial representations of data, provides an excellent way to do this.

Great Glyphs: All About Me provides ideas for making glyphs that link with students' personalities, preferences, and experiences. This gives students a familiar context for representing data—for example, in My Family Tree, children represent information about their families. You can connect these activities to various mathematics skills and concepts, as well as to other school disciplines. For example, Busy Around the Clock provides the perfect opportunity to reinforce time concepts with children, while Time to Read encourages children to read and enjoy books. All the glyphs include elements that emphasize individual preferences and information.

What Is a Glyph?

Just as a graph or Venn diagram conveys information about data that has been collected, a glyph displays information in the form of a picture. The word *glyph* comes from *hieroglyphics* (picture writing). The details of a glyph describe information about the person who created it. Each specific detail of a glyph provides the person viewing it with information. A legend allows students to see each feature of the glyph and what it represents.

For example, in Time to Read! the shape on the front cover of the book represents whether the student likes to read about animals, people, places, or another topic. If the student likes to read about animals, the shape is a square. If the student likes to read about people, the shape is a circle. A triangle indicates whether the student likes to read about places, and an oval conveys that the student likes to read about another topic. Other elements, such as the pattern on the back cover of the book, the color of the book, and the color and direction of the child's cap, represent other specific information.

Once students have completed their glyphs, encourage them to make observations about their own glyphs and those of their classmates. Invite them to discuss how their glyph is similar to or different from others. Have them note the attributes of a classmate's glyph and write about what they know about that person based on the glyph. See pages 8–9 for other ways to extend learning.

Introducing Glyphs to Students

These activities are designed for flexible use in the classroom. You might use the activities in any order, or create a glyph each month as part of your classroom routine. You might also use literature to introduce a glyph-making activity and generate interest in the particular topic. A list of related literature links is included for each glyph.

Each glyph in this book comes with reproducible templates. In advance, photocopy the pattern pages and legend and collect any other materials necessary for making the glyph. Review the directions and extension activities, and determine which of these you might use.

When you first introduce glyphs to students, begin by showing them a completed glyph. Then show them step-by-step how you used the legend to create the glyph. As you add each attribute to the glyph (such as the number of candles on a cake), ask students what this feature represents. It is important for students to make the connection that each attribute of the glyph represents information, or data.

One way to do this is by reproducing and distributing the legend page of each glyph activity. You can also copy the information onto a sheet of chart paper. Be sure to review the legend and the meaning of each feature with students before and after they create their own glyphs. For beginning readers, provide directions orally, one step at a time. You might show students how to use a blank sheet of paper to cover the legend steps. Sliding the paper down to reveal one step at a time will help students focus on reading small amounts of text.

Using Glyphs With English Language Learners

Students who repeatedly hear words in context are more likely to use them and understand their meaning. The activities in this book help give English language learners exposure to vocabulary such as geometry words (shape names, directionality and position words), measurement terms (months of the year, seasons, time), and number concepts (ordinality, cardinality, even and odd). Reviewing the directions and legend with students to introduce each activity and following up with a discussion and interpretation of the glyphs gives students even greater exposure to the vocabulary. As students compare the attributes of each glyph, they use number words, shape names, measurement terms, and more. This repeated exposure greatly benefits ELL students.

A Teacher-Student Dialogue

The following is an example of a classroom dialogue introducing glyphs to students for the first time. For each new glyph, modify the discussion to focus on the questions asked in the glyph-making activities and the responses students represent in their glyph. As you ask students questions, focus on mathematical concepts of the glyph rather than the craft-making aspect.

Teacher: (*holding up the completed birthday cake glyph so that the class can see it*) Children, look at this picture and think of something that you can say about what you see.

Student: You colored your birthday cake yellow.

Student: The cake has nine candles on it.

Student: All the candles are orange.

Student: Your cake is on a red plate.

Student: There are two kinds of shapes on your cake.

Student: The shapes make a pattern! There's one circle and two triangles, then one circle and two triangles.

Teacher: Wow, you noticed a lot about my birthday cake! All the attributes you just talked about tell something special about me. This birthday cake is a glyph. A glyph is a picture that tells information about the person who made it. Let's find out what that information is. (*Reveal the legend, one item at a time, pointing to each feature on the birthday cake glyph.*) This sheet is called the legend. The color of the cake tells you when in the month my birthday falls. The legend shows that if my birthday falls on a date between the first and the tenth day of the month, the cake is yellow. If the date of my birthday is between the eleventh and the twentieth day, the cake is blue. It is green if my birthday is a date between the twenty-first and the thirty-first. When in the month is my birthday?

Student: Your cake is yellow. That means your birthday is between the first and tenth day of the month.

Teacher: You're right! I colored my cake yellow because my birthday is on the fourth day of the month. What about the cake plate? What does the color of the plate tell us about whether I like ice cream with my cake? The legend shows that if the plate is red, I like ice cream with my cake. A purple plate means I don't like ice cream with my cake. Do I like ice cream with my cake?

Student: Yes! Your plate is red. You like ice cream with your birthday cake.

Teacher: Now let's look at the number of candles on my cake. What do they tell about me? Look at the legend and use that information to tell what you know about me based on the number of candles.

Student: You're older than nine years old. The legend shows that nine candles means that you're nine years old or older.

Teacher: Now look at the color of the candles. This will tell us in which season my birthday falls. If the candles are blue, it means my birthday is in the winter. If the candles are green, I have a spring birthday. Red candles mean I have a birthday in the summer, and orange candles mean my birthday is in the fall. In which season is my birthday?

Student: Your birthday is in the fall.

Teacher: How did you know that?

Student: You colored the candles on your cake orange. That means you have a fall birthday.

Teacher: That's right. My birthday is in November, and November is a fall month. Now look at the shapes on my cake. What does the order of these shapes tell you about the kind of cake I like best? The legend shows that if I like chocolate cake best, the circles and triangles will make an AB/AB pattern. How might this pattern look on the cake?

Student: You would put a circle, a triangle, a circle, a triangle, and keep going to the other end of the cake.

Teacher: That's right. Or I might use a triangle first, then a circle, and continue my pattern across the cake. Look at the legend again. It shows that if I like vanilla cake best, the circles and triangles will make an ABB/ABB pattern. How might the pattern on the cake look if I like vanilla cake best?

Student: Your cake would have a circle and two triangles, then a circle and two triangles. Or it could have a triangle and two circles, then a triangle and two circles.

Teacher: What does my cake tell you about what kind of cake I like best?

Student: Your cake shows that you like vanilla best because you made an ABB/ABB pattern. There's a circle, a triangle, a triangle, a circle, a triangle, and a triangle.

Teacher: Very good! Now let's review everything you know about me so far, based on the glyph I've made. (*Discuss the legend, and have students tell what they have learned.*) Remember that when you are trying to get information from a glyph, the legend reminds you what each part of the glyph represents. Now each of you will make glyphs about yourselves.

Making Glyphs With Students

After you have shown students an example of a completed glyph and reviewed the legend with them, begin by asking them to complete the first question on the legend. Remind students what information this attribute on the glyph will reveal. Wait for students to color, cut, and paste to complete the first question. Then hold up several glyphs in progress, one at a time, and ask the class to explain what each glyph tells so far about the child who made it. If you do this each time a new attribute is added, students will begin to grasp the concept that the attributes represent data. This also gives students a chance to practice analyzing the data shown on the glyph.

To make a glyph activity a rich and meaningful mathematics experience, rather than an arts and crafts project, encourage children to carefully consider each item on the legend before they select and add that attribute to their glyph. Remind students that each feature on their glyph should represent something about themselves—based on the legend.

Once the Glyph Is Complete— Extending Learning

Taking time to analyze the glyphs gives students a rich opportunity to build key math skills. For each glyph, you will find suggestions for critical-thinking activities and other extension activities that connect glyph-making to math concepts and to other areas of the curriculum. You will also find suggestions for books that explore the same themes as the glyphs. Use these to introduce or wrap up a glyph-making activity.

When students have completed their first glyph activity, ask them to work with a partner. Have each pair exchange their glyphs and tell a larger group or the whole class what they know about their partner based on the glyph. Older students can write these descriptions and then give them to their partner to read. As they talk and write, students are interpreting and analyzing data.

Another follow-up activity is to brainstorm ways to sort the completed glyphs. Divide the class into small groups and have each group determine how they will sort their glyphs. For example, they might sort the Happy Birthday to Me! glyphs by the number of candles or by the color of the plate. As each group reports to the class, ask them to show the sorting method, and then discuss the data that is revealed by each way of sorting. Since each glyph has many different attributes, each can be sorted in a variety of ways. Keeping the glyphs sorted, display them on a bulletin board with the question "How did we sort our glyphs?" Invite students from other classrooms to interpret the data.

With any glyph activity, students can write a story or poem, draw or write about their glyph and their findings in their math journals, or extend the glyph with other symbols to represent additional information.

Feel free to modify elements of the glyphs as needed to make them more appropriate for your students. We have found these activities highly motivating to students—and students' use of mathematics vocabulary improves as they create glyphs and interpret the data revealed in them. Enjoy!

Connections to the NCTM Standards

The activities in this book correspond to the standards recommended by the National Council of Teachers of Mathematics (NCTM).

Glyph Activity	Content Standards					Process Standards				
	Number and Operations	Algebra	Geometry	Measurement	Data Analysis and Probability	Problem Solving	Reasoning and Proof	Communication	Connections	Representation
Busy Around the Clock	●		●	●	●	●	●	●	●	●
My Family Tree	●		●		●	●	●	●	●	●
Happy Birthday to Me!	●	●	●		●	●	●	●	●	●
Time to Read!			●	●	●	●	●	●	●	●
School Is Cool!	●			●	●	●	●	●	●	●
Thinking About Home	●		●		●	●	●	●	●	●
Mystery Critter Crate	●	●	●		●	●	●	●	●	●
My Favorite Food	●		●		●	●	●	●	●	●
Time to Play			●	●	●	●	●	●	●	●
Sports Jersey	●		●		●	●	●	●	●	●
Weather Window	●		●	●	●	●	●	●	●	●
A Sunny Future for Me		●	●		●	●	●	●	●	●

Busy Around the Clock

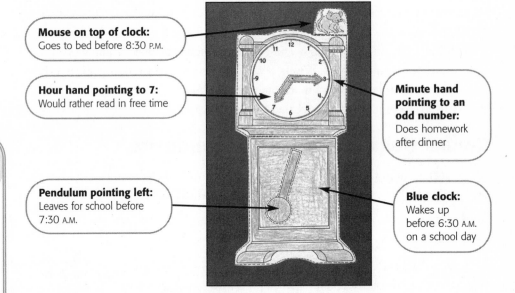

Mouse on top of clock:
Goes to bed before 8:30 P.M.

Hour hand pointing to 7:
Would rather read in free time

Pendulum pointing left:
Leaves for school before 7:30 A.M.

Minute hand pointing to an odd number:
Does homework after dinner

Blue clock:
Wakes up before 6:30 A.M. on a school day

Math Skills

- time

- directionality: left, right, middle, top, bottom

- reading numbers

- even and odd numbers

Materials

- reproducible glyph patterns and legend (pages 12–14)

- completed clock glyph

- 12- by 18-inch construction paper

- scissors

- glue or paste

- crayons

Creating the Glyph

1. Distribute copies of the clock glyph patterns and legend to students. Review the legend, one characteristic at a time, as you display a glyph you have completed. Then distribute the other materials, and invite students to use the legend to create their own personal clock glyph.

2. To begin, have students cut out the patterns. Show them how to glue the top and bottom sections of their clock patterns onto a sheet of construction paper, positioned vertically.

3. As students work on the first question on the legend, direct them to color only the outside of the clock, leaving the clock face white.

Critical Thinking

Display the completed glyphs in two groups: those with the mouse on top of the clock and those with the mouse on the bottom. Ask students to determine how the glyphs were sorted. What information does this show about each group? Then have students in each group put their glyphs in order by the time shown on the clocks. (To simplify, assume they are all either A.M. or P.M.) Ask students to interpret the data on each glyph and share what it shows about the person who created that glyph. Have students compare the glyphs in their group to find similarities and differences in their daily schedules.

Explore More

Math   Give students each a blank index card. Tell them that the card represents the window on a digital clock. Ask students to write on their cards the digital time that represents the same time shown on their clock glyphs. Then spread out all the glyphs on one table and the digital time cards on another. Invite students to take turns picking a time card and then searching the glyphs to find the clock with the matching time.

Math   Have students solve problems using the time shown on their clock glyphs. For example, you might ask students to find the clock that shows 4:35 on it. Then, after they locate the correct clock, ask them to tell what time the clock would show if it was set for one hour later or two hours earlier. Or you might have them locate two clocks that show different times and then find the difference between those two times.

Social Studies, Math   Discuss with students the kinds of activities they do after school. Then ask them to write a schedule to show what their individual schedules look like from the time they leave school until the time they go to bed. When finished, have students compare their schedules to find out how many eat dinner, do homework, read, and so on, at the same time. To extend, have students compute how much time passes between each activity shown on their schedules.

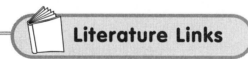

Literature Links

Bats Around the Clock
by Kathi Appelt (HarperCollins, 2000).
American Batstand dance marathon is in full swing.

Boom Chicka Rock
by John Archambault (Philomel Books, 2004).
The mice bravely leave their cuckoo clock home to stir up a party complete with cake and lively dancing. But can they make it back to the clock before midnight—and without waking up the cat?

Time to . . .
by Bruce McMillan
(Lothrop, Lee and Shepard, 1989).
Readers follow the activities of a young boy throughout the day through photo-illustrations and both analog and digital clocks that mark the passing hours.

Busy Around the Clock

(1) When do you wake up on a school day?

	before 6:30 A.M.	between 6:30 A.M. and 7:00 A.M.	after 7:00 A.M.
Color of Clock	blue	red	green

(2) When do you leave for school?

	before 7:30 A.M.	at 7:30 A.M.	after 7:30 A.M.
Position of Pendulum	left	middle	right

(3) What would you rather do in your free time?

	play outside	play a game	read a book	another activity
Position of Hour Hand	1 or 2	4 or 5	7 or 8	10 or 11

(4) When do you do your homework?

	before dinner	after dinner
Position of Minute Hand	any even number	any odd number

(5) When do you go to bed on a school night?

	before 8:30 P.M.	8:30 P.M. or later
Position of Mouse	top of clock	bottom of clock

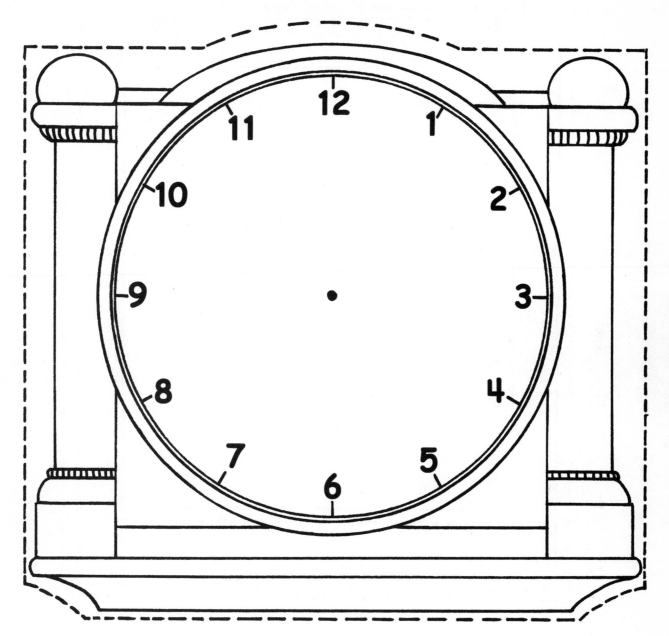

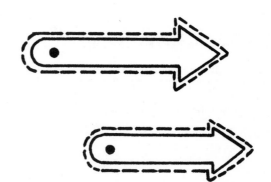

My Family Tree

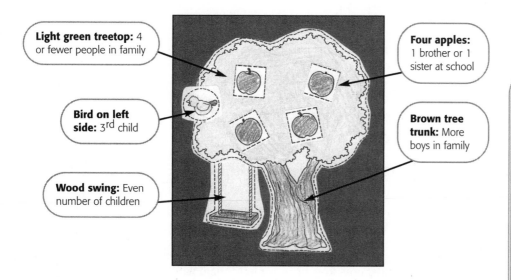

Light green treetop: 4 or fewer people in family

Four apples: 1 brother or 1 sister at school

Bird on left side: 3rd child

Brown tree trunk: More boys in family

Wood swing: Even number of children

Math Skills

- counting
- greater than, less than, equal to
- even and odd numbers
- one-to-one correspondence
- ordinal numbers
- directionality: above, below, left, right

Creating the Glyph

1. Distribute copies of the family tree glyph patterns and the legend to students. Review the legend, one characteristic at a time, as you display a glyph you have completed. Then distribute the other materials, and invite students to use the legend to create their own personal family tree glyph.

2. To start, have students cut out the patterns and glue their tree onto a sheet of construction paper, positioned vertically.

3. Instruct students to include themselves when they answer questions 1, 2, and 3. Encourage students to count anyone they consider family—this might be their immediate family, extended family, people who live with them, and so on. For question 3, have students glue the swing to the left side of the tree.

Critical Thinking

Use students' glyphs to create logic problems. Give clues based on a glyph's features and then have students "guess the glyph." For example:

> My *treetop is light green, and my trunk is tan.*
> *I have a tire swing hanging on me.*
> *I have five apples.*
> *A bird is sitting on top of me.*
> *Which tree am I?*

Materials

- reproducible glyph patterns and legend (pages 17–19)
- completed family tree glyph
- 9- by 12-inch construction paper
- scissors
- glue or paste
- crayons

15

Ask students what each of these features represents about the person who created the glyph. Or provide higher-order thinking problems by naming what each feature represents. For the same glyph above, you might give these clues:

There are four or fewer people in my family.
There are more girls than boys in my family.
There is an odd number of children in my family.
I have no brothers or sisters at this school.
I am the first child in my family.
Which tree am I?

Explore More

Social Studies, Math Invite students to create a time line of their lives. Have them include important events such as their birth date, first steps, first words, and first day of school, as well as personal accomplishments such as learning to ride a bike and writing their name. Encourage students to add illustrations to their time lines. To show students an example of a time line, you might create one based on important events in your own life to share with the class.

Language Arts Invite students to write about a favorite family memory. It could be a daily routine, such as walking the dog with a parent, or a special event, such as celebrating a family member's birthday. First, have students complete a story map to show the beginning, middle, and end of their stories. You might give a short lesson on using quotation marks, and encourage students to include dialogue in their stories.

Social Studies Have students create a family tree to represent the relationship between themselves, their parents, and their siblings. Students can draw a picture of each family member and then write his or her name and age (or birthday). To extend, they might also include grandparents, aunts, uncles, and cousins on their family tree.

 Literature Links

I Love My Family by Wade Hudson (Scholastic, 1993). A young boy shares about the good times he has at a family reunion.

Me and My Family Tree by Joan Sweeney (Crown Publishers, 1999). A child uses a tree to show how everyone in her family is related to her.

The Relatives Came by Cynthia Rylant (Bradbury Press, 1985). When relatives from Virginia come to visit during the summer, a family's home is filled with wonderful, memorable experiences.

Name _____

My Family Tree

1 How many people are in your family?

Color of Treetop	4 or fewer people	5 or more people
	light green	dark green

2 Are there more boys or girls in your family?

Color of Tree Trunk	more boys	more girls	equal number of boys and girls
	brown	tan	gray

3 Count the number of children in your family. Is the number even or odd?

Type of Swing	even number	odd number
	wood swing	tire swing

4 How many brothers or sisters do you have at this school?

Number of Apples in Tree	none	1 brother or 1 sister	more than 1 brother or sister
	5	4	3

5 What is your birth order in your family?

Position of Bird	1st child	2nd child	3rd child	4th child or later
	top of tree	bottom of tree	left side of tree	right side of tree

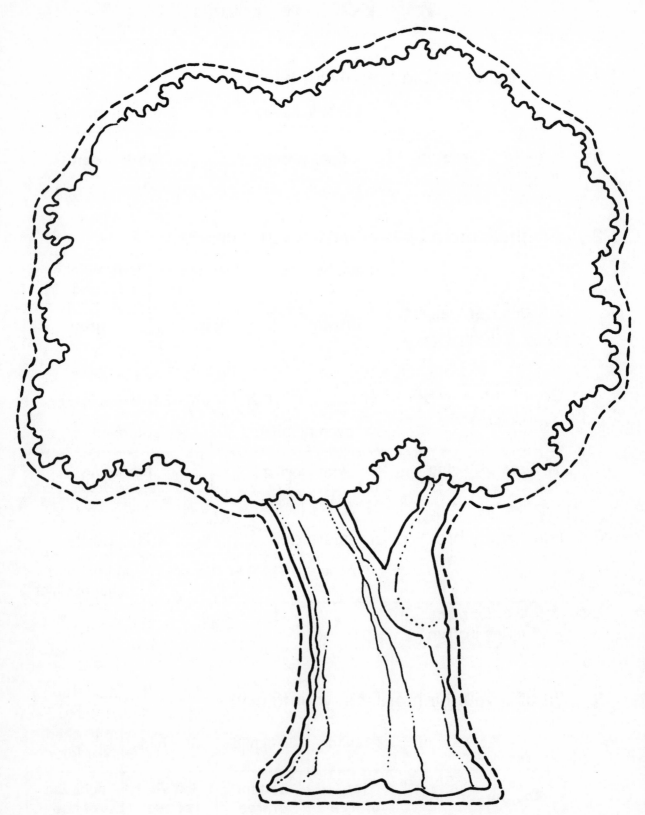

18

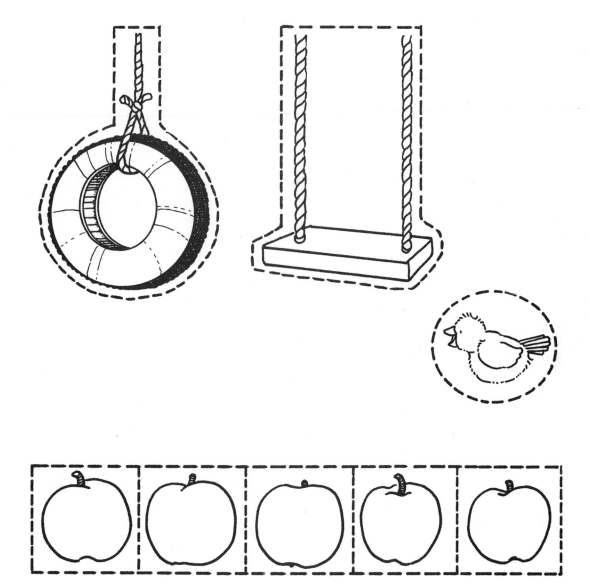

Happy Birthday to Me!

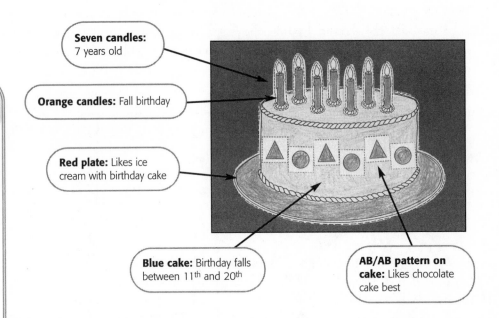

Seven candles: 7 years old

Orange candles: Fall birthday

Red plate: Likes ice cream with birthday cake

Blue cake: Birthday falls between 11th and 20th

AB/AB pattern on cake: Likes chocolate cake best

Math Skills

- ordinal numbers

- counting

- concepts of time: seasons and calendar

- one-to-one correspondence

- patterns

- geometry: shapes

Materials

- reproducible glyph patterns and legend (pages 22–24)

- completed birthday cake glyph

- 9- by 12-inch construction paper

- scissors

- glue or paste

- crayons

Creating the Glyph

Distribute copies of the birthday cake glyph patterns and legend to students. Review the legend, one characteristic at a time, as you display a glyph you have completed. Then distribute the other materials, and invite students to use the legend to create their own personal birthday cake glyph. If desired, have students glue or paste their glyph onto construction paper for a sturdy backing.

Critical Thinking

Have students group themselves according to the season in which their birthdays fall (candle color). Then ask each group of students to write their birthdays (month and date) on sticky notes, stick them on their glyph, and arrange their glyphs in order by the month of their birthdays. Next, have students form three groups, according to when in the month they have a birthday (cake color).

Ask students questions about the members of their groups, and have them look at the glyphs to find the information. For example, how many people in your group are six years old or younger? Seven years old? Do more people in your group prefer chocolate or vanilla cake? Encourage students to compare the data on the glyphs to discover their similarities and differences.

Explore More

Math   Display all the glyphs that show candles of the same color. Ask students to count the candles on these glyphs. Then have a volunteer write that number on chart paper, using a crayon that matches the candle color. After the candle count has been recorded for each candle color, have students compare the numbers to discover which color has the most candles and which has the fewest candles. For each comparison that the class makes, invite a student to write a corresponding number sentence using the signs for greater than, fewer than, and equal to.

Math   Work with students to create a class graph of their birthdays. To make the graph, divide a lined sheet of chart paper into 12 columns. Write the name of a different month at the top of each column. Then, working from the bottom of the chart to the top, have students write their name under the month in which their birthday falls. When finished, examine the graph with the class to find out in which month students have the most or fewest birthdays, or the same number of birthdays. You might also ask students to tell what day of the month their birthday falls on. Do any two students in the class share a birthday?

Language Arts   Invite students to write about their best birthday ever. Encourage them to include details about the setting (time and place), the events of the day, the people they spent the day with, and other important information. You might discuss sensory descriptions with students and guide them to include descriptions of the sights, sounds, smells, and so on.

Literature Links

Birthday Presents
by Cynthia Rylant (Orchard Books, 1987).
The parents of a young girl share the tears, trials, and triumphs of the first six years of her life. Illustrated to resemble a family album, this book inspires readers to reflect on their own family history and memories.

Happy Birthday, Moon
by Frank Asch (Prentice-Hall, 1982).
Bear wants to get the moon a birthday present, but he's not sure what to get it. That is, until he discovers that the moon wants the same thing he wants—a hat!

The Secret Birthday Message
by Eric Carle (Crowell, 1972).
On his birthday, a boy receives a secret message that leads him on an adventure through fun-shaped pages to search for his birthday surprise.

Some Birthday!
by Patricia Polacco (Simon & Schuster, 1991).
Convinced that her family has forgotten her birthday, Patricia agrees to go along with Dad and Rich to see the monster at Clay Pit Bottom. Little does she know that the scariest place in town holds the most exciting birthday adventure ever!

Happy Birthday to Me!

1 When in the month does your birthday fall?

	1st–10th	11th–20th	21st–31st
Color of Cake	yellow	blue	green

2 Do you like ice cream with birthday cake?

	yes	no
Color of Plate	red	purple

3 How old are you?

	6 years old or younger	7 years old	8 years old	9 years old or older
Number of Candles	six	seven	eight	nine

4 In which season is your birthday?

	winter	spring	summer	fall
Color of Candles	blue	green	red	orange

5 What kind of cake do you like best? Glue circles and triangles to make a pattern.

	chocolate	vanilla
Pattern on Cake	AB/AB pattern	ABB/ABB pattern

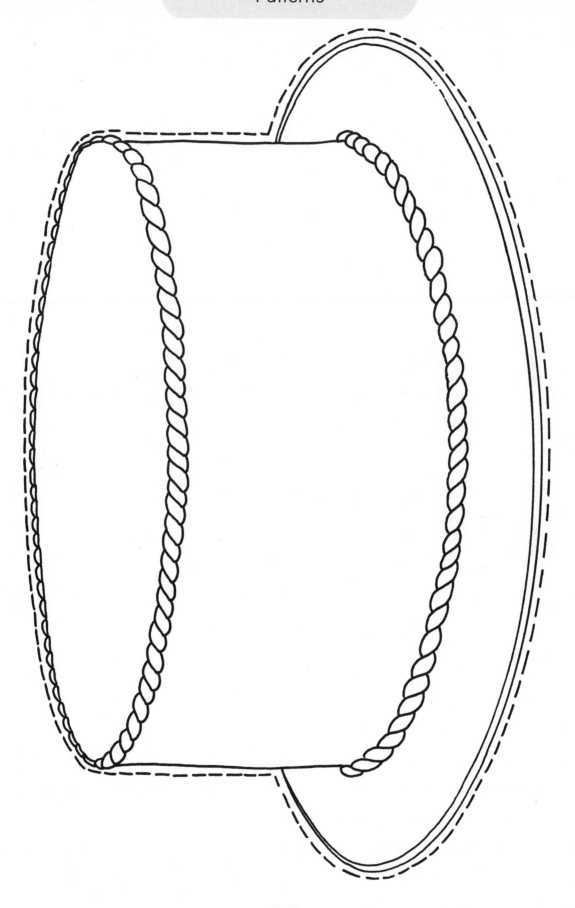

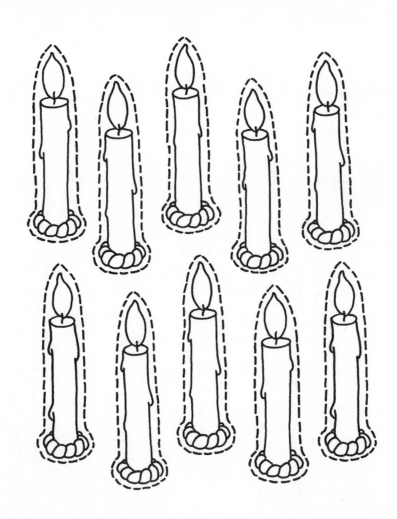

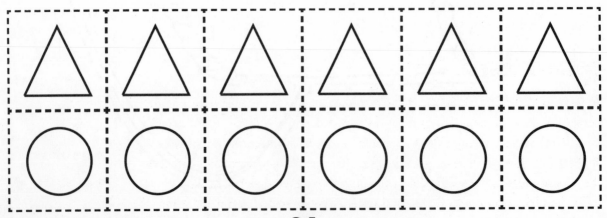

Time to Read!

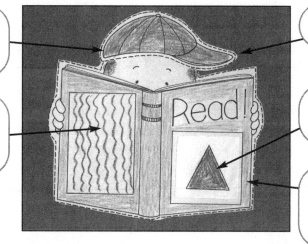

Purple cap: Favorite place to read is at home

Wavy lines on back cover: Likes to read in the evening

Right-facing cap: Likes fiction best

Triangle on front cover: Favorite topic to read about is places

Red book: Favorite place to find a book is classroom library

Creating the Glyph

Distribute copies of the reader glyph patterns and the legend to students. Review the legend, one characteristic at a time, as you display a glyph you have completed. Then distribute the other materials, and invite students to use the legend to create their own personal reader glyph.

Critical Thinking

Choose one attribute and arrange some of the completed reader glyphs in an AB/AB pattern. For example, use the color of the cap and make a green/purple/green/purple pattern. Have students look at the glyphs and identify the pattern. Then ask them to select a glyph that would extend the pattern. Ask students what these glyphs represent about the students who made them (their favorite places to read are at school and at home). Repeat the activity with another attribute to create another pattern, such as ABC/ABC, using the shape on the front cover of the book or the design on the back cover.

Explore More

Math, Language Arts Ask students to write the title of their favorite book on a sheet of paper. Then have them count and record how many times each letter appears in the title. For example, in *The Three Bears*, the letter *t* appears two times, *h* two times, and *e* four times. Afterward, have students count the total number of letters in the title. Then show them how to use their individual letter counts with the total letter count to write fractions. As they

Math Skills

- geometry: shapes
- time concepts: time of day
- patterns
- directionality: left, right

Materials

- reproducible glyph patterns and legend (pages 27–29)
- completed reader glyph
- scissors
- glue or paste
- crayons

work, encourage students to say each fraction as they write it and to explain what the numbers mean. For instance, a student might write the fraction $^4/_{13}$ and then explain that the 4 represents how many times the letter *e* appears in the title and that 13 is the total number of letters in the title.

Language Arts, Math Create a two-column chart labeled with the headings "Fiction" and "Nonfiction." Explain to students the difference between the two. Then ask students to write the title of their favorite book on a sticky note. Is the book fiction or nonfiction? Have students attach their sticky notes to the column that best describes the category that the book belongs to. When finished, count the number of sticky notes in each column to discover whether more of students' favorite books are fiction or nonfiction. Compare the totals in each column.

Language Arts During a designated week, read a variety of fiction and nonfiction books to students. After each reading, discuss what category the book belongs to. Encourage students to tell why each book is either fiction or nonfiction. At the end of the week, tell students that they will create their own books to add to the class library. Have them choose a topic and then decide whether they want to write a fiction or a nonfiction book. If a student chooses to write a nonfiction book, encourage him or her to use other book resources or the Internet to find and verify facts for the topic. After students write, illustrate, and bind their books, invite them to share the books with the class. Then place the books in the class library for students to enjoy during reading and free choice activity times.

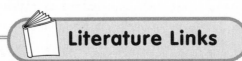

Literature Links

Aunt Chip and the Great Triple Creek Dam Affair
by Patricia Polacco
(Philomel Books, 1996).
After spending 50 years in bed, Aunt Chip jumps to action when she realizes the people in her town can't read. With the help of some avid new readers, a fallen TV tower, and her librarian know-how, Aunt Chip turns the townspeople away from their TVs and sparks the love of literature in them.

The Wednesday Surprise
by Eve Bunting (Clarion Books, 1989).
Every Wednesday night, Grandma and Anna enjoy special times as they read together and prepare for a big birthday surprise. And what a surprise it is when the family learns that Anna is teaching her Grandma to read!

Wild About Books
by Judy Sierra (Knopf, 2004).
When librarian Molly McGrew mistakenly drives the bookmobile into a zoo, the animals go wild over the wonderful books she introduces them to.

Time to Read!

1 What is your favorite topic to read about?

	animals	people	places	another topic
Shape on Front Cover	square	circle	triangle	oval

2 When do you like to read? Draw a design on the back cover.

	in the morning	in the afternoon	in the evening	any time of day
Design on Back Cover	° ° ° °	///////	}}}}}}	✳ ✳ ✳ ✳

3 What is your favorite place to find a book?

	school library	classroom library	public library	another place
Color of Book	blue	red	yellow	orange

4 Which kind of book do you like best?

	fiction	nonfiction
Direction of Kid's Cap	right	left

5 Where is your favorite place to read?

	at school	at home	another place
Color of Cap	green	purple	red

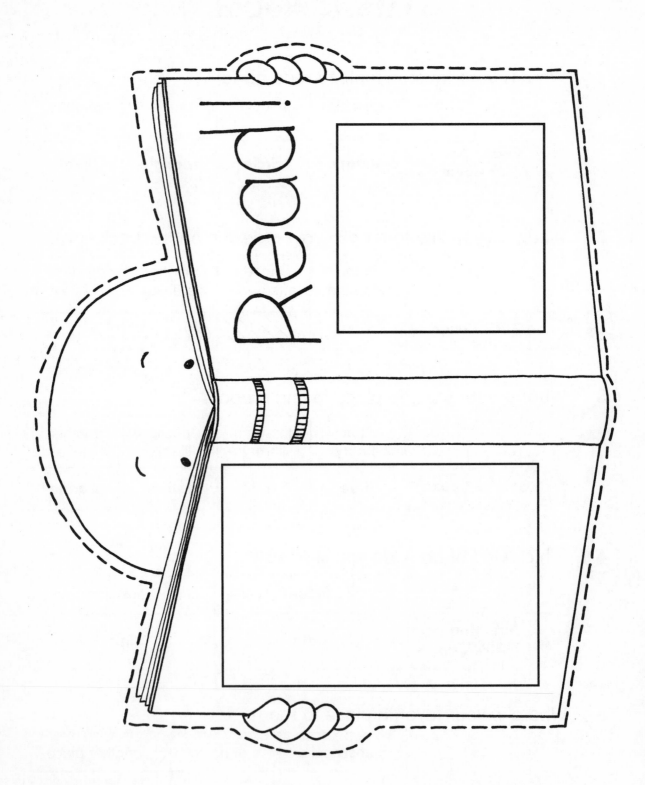

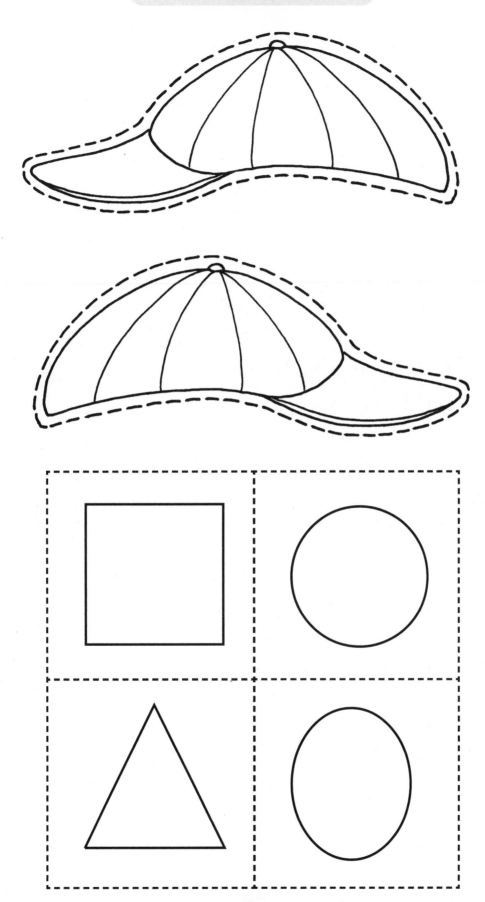

School Is Cool!

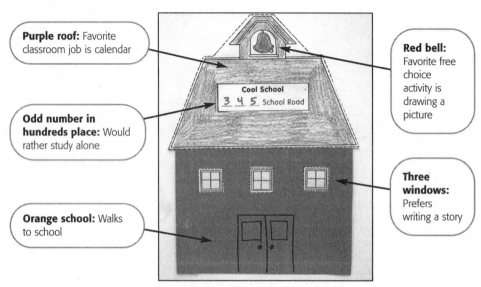

Purple roof: Favorite classroom job is calendar

Odd number in hundreds place: Would rather study alone

Orange school: Walks to school

Red bell: Favorite free choice activity is drawing a picture

Three windows: Prefers writing a story

Cool School

3 4 5 School Road

Math Skills

- counting
- one-to-one correspondence
- writing numerals
- even and odd numbers
- place value

Materials

- reproducible glyph patterns and legend (pages 32–33)
- completed schoolhouse glyph
- 8- by 6-inch red, blue, orange, and yellow construction paper
- rulers
- scissors
- glue or paste
- crayons

Creating the Glyph

1. Distribute copies of the schoolhouse glyph patterns and the legend to students. Review the legend, one characteristic at a time, as you display a glyph you have completed. Then distribute the other materials, and invite students to use the legend to create their own personal schoolhouse glyph.

2. Have students choose the color of construction paper that corresponds to their answer to question 1. Students will use this piece, positioned horizontally, for schoolhouse building. Have students glue or tape the roof to the construction paper. For question 5, students write a three-digit number on the sign.

3. Invite students to add a door to their schoolhouse glyph.

Critical Thinking

Display all the glyphs on a wall or bulletin board, and divide the class into small groups. Then ask students which part of the schoolhouse glyph identifies everyone's favorite free choice activity at school (the color of the bell). Instruct students in each group to share their ideas about how they might create a graph to represent this information. (Each group will graph the data from the entire class.) Encourage group members to agree on what kind of graph they would like to make, such as a vertical or horizontal graph with bars, symbols, or pictures. When finished, invite groups to share their graphs with the class. Discuss the fact that all the graphs represent the same data.

Explore More

Math Invite students to put the glyphs in order by the number shown on the school sign. Before they begin, have students decide whether to sequence the glyphs from the lowest number to the highest or the highest to lowest. This is a good opportunity to discuss place value and ask students how they can tell that numbers are higher or lower than others. To extend, challenge students to sort the glyphs into two groups according to whether the number on the sign is an even or odd number. Then have them order the glyphs in each group from lowest to highest or highest to lowest.

Math Have students add the three digits in the sign on their glyph and then write the sum on a sticky note. Next, call out any number that comes to mind. Then ask students to tell whether the number on their paper is greater than or less than the named number. Or have them add the new number to the number on their paper and write the sum. Students might also create subtraction problems or write number comparison sentences using the two numbers.

Language Arts, Math Ask students to write a description of the inside of their classroom (or another room at school). Encourage them to use positional words and phrases to help describe where items are located in the classroom. If desired, label large index cards with terms such *on top of, under, beside, to the left of,* and *to the right of.* Then display the cards in the writing center so that students can refer to them as they write their descriptions.

Language Arts, Social Studies, Art Discuss with students the many great things about their school. Record these on a sheet of chart paper. Then invite students to create brochures, posters, and flyers that highlight some of their favorite school programs, classes, and so on. Display students' work in the hallway for other classes and visitors to enjoy.

Literature Links

The Bug in Teacher's Coffee and Other School Poems
by Kalli Dakos. (HarperCollins, 1999).
Inanimate objects take on a personality of their own in this collection of simple poems in which the world is seen from the perspective of common, everyday school items.

Hello School! A Classroom Full of Poems
by Dee Lillegard (Alfred A. Knopf, 2001).
Colorful 3-D pictures and short rhyming text help bring the classroom to life in the 38 poems that celebrate school in this book.

School Is Cool!

1 How do you get to school?

	ride a bus	ride in a car	walk	another way
Color of School	red	blue	orange	yellow

2 What is your favorite classroom job?

	line leader	messenger	calendar	another job
Color of Roof	brown	black	purple	gray

3 Which activity do you prefer?

	reading a story	listening to a story	writing a story
Number of Windows	5	4	3

4 What is your favorite free choice activity at school?

	reading a book	playing a board game	drawing a picture	another activity
Color of Bell	yellow	orange	red	pink

5 Would you rather study by yourself or with a partner?

	by myself	with a partner
Three-Digit Number on Sign	odd number in hundreds place	even number in hundreds place

Great Glyphs: All About Me   Scholastic Teaching Resources, page 32

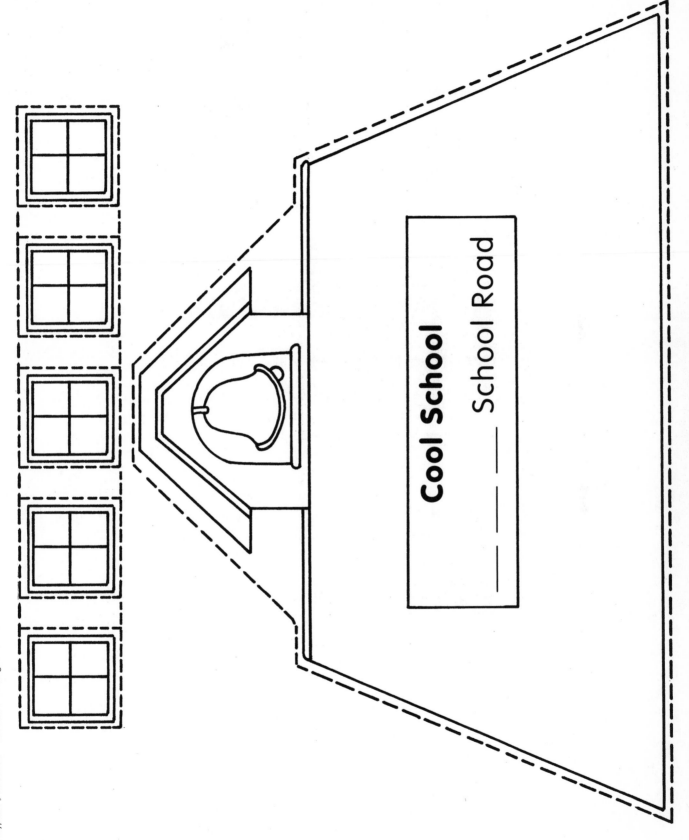

Cool School

School Road

Thinking About Home

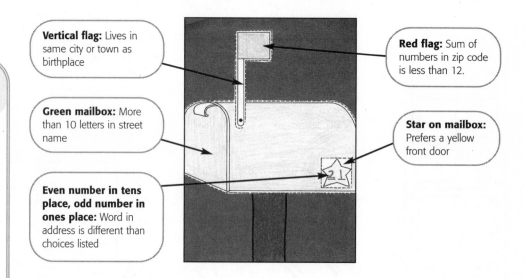

Vertical flag: Lives in same city or town as birthplace

Red flag: Sum of numbers in zip code is less than 12.

Green mailbox: More than 10 letters in street name

Star on mailbox: Prefers a yellow front door

Even number in tens place, odd number in ones place: Word in address is different than choices listed

Math Skills

- counting
- greater than, less than, equal to
- addition
- geometry: shapes
- place value
- even and odd numbers
- directionality: vertical, horizontal

Materials

- reproducible glyph patterns and legend (pages 36–37)
- completed mailbox glyph
- 9- by12-inch construction paper
- scissors
- glue or paste
- crayons

Creating the Glyph

1. Distribute copies of the mailbox glyph patterns and the legend to students. Review the legend, one characteristic at a time, as you display a glyph you have completed. Then distribute the other materials, and invite students to use the legend to create their own personal mailbox glyph.

2. For question 1, have students use the name of the street in their address. Have them include words such as *street*, *road*, and *lane* as part of the name. For question 3, have students line up the dots to attach the flag. For question 5, students write a two-digit number on the shape.

3. Have students glue their glyph onto a sheet of construction paper positioned vertically and draw a post.

Critical Thinking

Choose several glyphs to examine as a class. Have students look at the number on the mailbox. Direct their attention to the number in the tens place. Is it even or odd? Group the glyphs together that have an odd number in the tens place. What does this show about the students' addresses? (They have the word *street* or *lane* in it.) Then divide these glyphs into two groups: those with an odd number in the ones place and those with an even number in the ones place. What does this tell about the students' addresses? Extend by looking at the glyphs with an even number in the tens place.

Explore More

Math   Ask students to write on an index card the number of their street address. Then invite them to sort themselves into groups according to different criteria related to their number. For example, you might have all students with two-digit numbers form one group, three-digit numbers form another group, and so on. Or you might have students sort themselves into groups according to whether their numbers are odd or even. Alternatively, they might add all the digits in their numbers and then sort themselves into groups by increments of ten (teens, 20s, 30s, and so on).

Language Arts   Teach students the correct way to address an envelope, and review ways to write greetings and closings in a letter. Set up a mail center in your classroom with a mailbox for each student (ask families to send in empty shoe boxes). Have students write an imaginary address on their mailbox. Provide students with envelopes and plain paper for stationery. Encourage them to write letters to classmates, address them to the invented address, and deliver them to their classroom mailboxes.

Social Studies   Provide students with a large sheet of craft paper, markers, and crayons. Invite them to draw a map of an imaginary town or city. Encourage students to draw a street and name it after themselves. Then have them add places they might find in a town or city, such as a post office, bank, and playground. Next, have students work with a partner and ask each other for directions to get from place to place. For example, one student might ask, "How do I get from the library to the supermarket?" The other student might answer, "Take a left on Simon Street, then make a right on Eduardo Avenue."

Literature Links

A House for Hermit Crab
by Eric Carle (Picture Book Studio, 1987).
When Hermit Crab finds a new shell, he feels his new home is unwelcoming. But with the help of his friends, the crab soon has a cozy, comfortable home.

This Is My House
by Arthur Dorros (Scholastic, 1992).
Interesting text and pictures take readers on a worldwide trip to learn about the types of houses people live in, how they are built, and more.

Yours Truly, Goldilocks
by Alma Flor Ada
(Atheneum Books for Young Readers, 1998).
The three little pigs send invitations for a housewarming party to their fairyland friends. But while the characters are busy exchanging messages through the mail, two sly wolves are up to some tricks of their own.

Thinking About Home

1 How many letters are in your street name?

	fewer than 10	exactly 10	more than 10
Color of Mailbox	blue	purple	green

2 Add the numbers in your zip code. What is the sum?

	less than 12	exactly 12	more than 12
Color of Flag	red	orange	yellow

3 Do you live in the same city or town in which you were born?

	yes	no
Position of Flag	vertical	horizontal

4 Which color front door would you rather have?

	blue	orange	yellow	another color
Shape on Mailbox	circle	triangle	star	square

5 Which word is in your address?

	street	road	lane	another word
Two-Digit Number on Shape	tens place— odd ones place— odd	tens place— even ones place— even	tens place— odd ones place— even	tens place— even ones place— odd

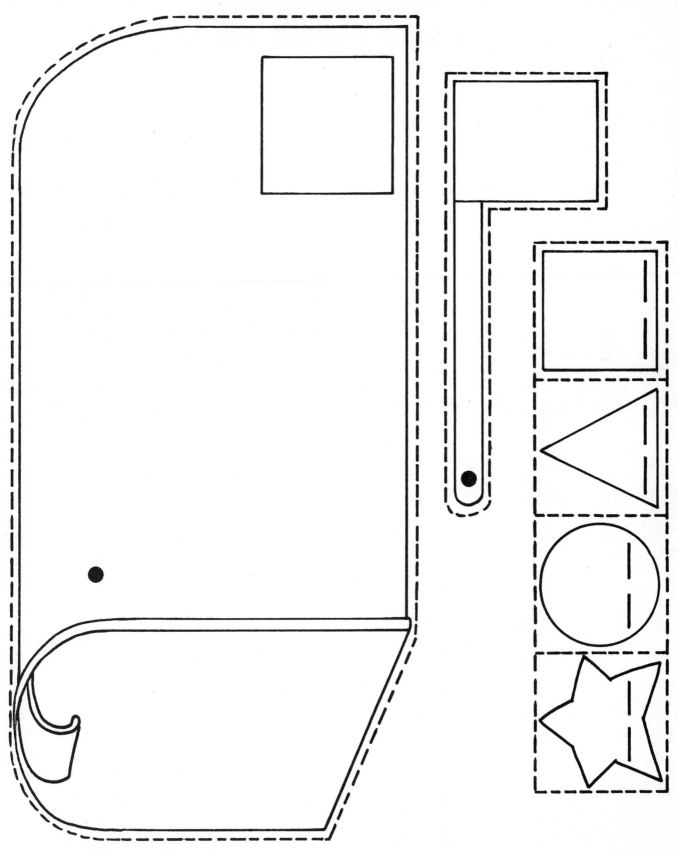

Mystery Critter Crate

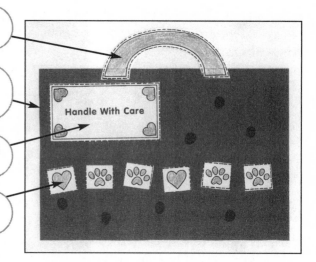

Round handle: Favorite animal has 2 legs

Red crate: Number of letters in favorite animal's name when doubled is more than 10

Sign in top left corner: Favorite animal flies

ABB/ABB pattern on crate: Favorite animal has feathers

Handle With Care

Math Skills

- counting

- multiplication

- directionality: top, bottom, left, right

- patterns

Materials

- reproducible glyph patterns and legend (pages 40–41)

- completed critter crate glyph

- 6- by 9-inch yellow, orange, and red construction paper

- scissors

- glue or paste

- crayons

Creating the Glyph

1. Distribute copies of the critter crate patterns and the legend to students. Review the legend, one characteristic at a time, as you display a glyph you have completed. Then distribute the other materials, and invite students to use the legend to create their own critter crate glyph.

2. Have students choose the color of construction paper that corresponds to their answer to question 1. Have students glue the handle to the construction paper "crate." Invite students to draw a few black circles on their crate for air holes.

3. Once students have completed their glyph, invite them to draw a picture of their favorite animal on the back of the glyph.

Critical Thinking

Select six of the completed critter crate glyphs and sort them into two groups. Ask students to guess the rule by looking for the attribute that is common to all the critter crates in one of the groups. The attribute (or attributes) could be that the sign is in the top left corner (the animal flies) or the crates have a trapezoid-shaped handle (students' favorite pet has four legs). Fewer attributes or more obvious attributes will make it easier for students to analyze the grouping and guess the rule.

Explore More

Math   Use the glyphs to reinforce simple multiplication. First, have students sort all the glyphs by the number of legs that their favorite animal has. (Group glyphs together by the shape of the handle.) Ask them to count all the glyphs in the group representing animals with zero legs. Then have them multiply that number by the number of legs to find out how many legs the animals have in all (in this case, the answer is zero). Instruct students to repeat the activity for the glyphs representing animals with two legs, and then four legs.

Language Arts   Display the glyphs and challenge students to guess the animals. Turn over the glyphs to reveal the answers. Invite students to pretend that they are their favorite animal. Where would they live? What would they eat? How would they move about? What makes them so interesting? After students have thought about the answers to these questions, ask them to write about their experiences as their favorite animal. Encourage them to include informative details about the animal throughout their piece. When finished, have them illustrate their work and share it with the class.

Social Studies, Language Arts   Invite students to share their pet care knowledge by making "How to Care for a . . ." booklets. First, ask them to write the title on a construction paper cover, filling in the name of an animal. Then have students write on separate sheets of paper a helpful tip, piece of advice, or directions related to caring for that specific animal. Encourage them to use illustrations, diagrams, and other picture representations to make their booklets more interesting and informative. You might have students research information to include in their booklets. Invite students to share their books with classmates, and then add them to the class library.

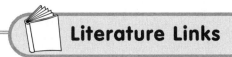

Literature Links

Franklin Wants a Pet
by Paulette Bourgeois (Scholastic, 1995).
Franklin chooses a goldfish for his first pet.

Laura Numeroff's 10-Step Guide to Living With Your Monster
by Laura Numeroff (Laura Geringer, 2002).
This humorous book provides hints on how to care for a pet monster.

Pet Show!
by Ezra Jack Keats (Macmillan, 1972).
When Archie's cat runs away, he surprises everyone by entering a "germ" in the neighborhood pet show.

Mystery Critter Crate

1 Count the number of letters in your favorite animal's name. Double the number.

	fewer than 10	exactly 10	more than 10
Color of Crate	yellow	orange	red

2 How many legs does your favorite animal have?

	0 legs	2 legs	4 legs	more than 4 legs
Shape of Handle				

3 How does your favorite animal usually move?

	flies	swims	walks	another way
Position of Sign	top left corner	bottom left corner	top right corner	bottom right corner

4 What does your favorite animal have on its body? Glue on paw prints and hearts to make a pattern.

	fur	feathers	scales	something else
Pattern on Crate	AB/AB	ABB/ABB	AAB/AAB	ABA/ABA

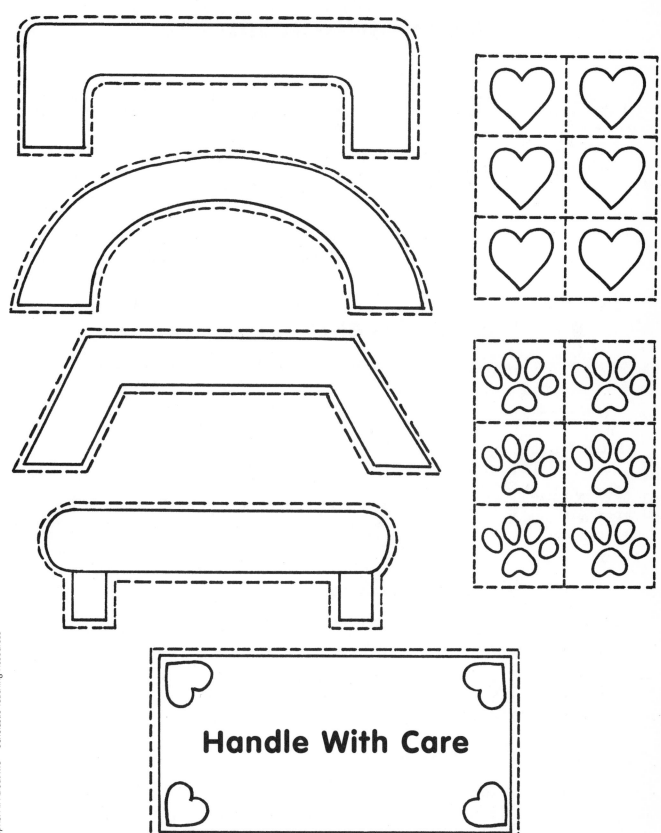

Handle With Care

My Favorite Food

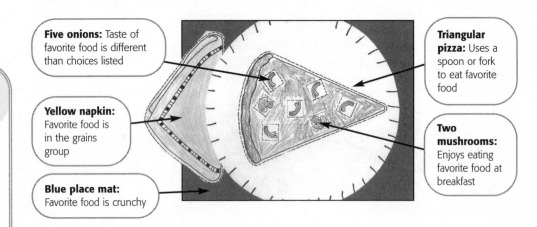

Five onions: Taste of favorite food is different than choices listed

Yellow napkin: Favorite food is in the grains group

Blue place mat: Favorite food is crunchy

Triangular pizza: Uses a spoon or fork to eat favorite food

Two mushrooms: Enjoys eating favorite food at breakfast

Math Skills

- geometry: shapes
- counting
- one-to-one correspondence
- greater than, less than, equal to

Materials

- reproducible glyph patterns and legend (pages 44–46)
- completed pizza glyph
- 9- by 12-inch green, red, blue, and orange construction paper
- 9-inch paper plates or paper circles
- scissors
- glue or paste
- crayons

Creating the Glyph

1. Distribute copies of the pizza glyph patterns and the legend to students. Review the legend, one characteristic at a time, as you display a glyph you have completed. Then distribute the other materials, and invite students to use the legend to create their own personal pizza glyph.

2. For question 1, students glue their pizza onto a paper circle or plate.

3. For question 4, have students choose construction paper of the color that corresponds to their answer. Instruct students to glue their plate and napkin onto the construction paper, overlapping them to fit.

Critical Thinking

Review with students the information shown on the glyphs. Then ask them what other questions they could ask about their favorite food. For example, they might ask, "How often do you eat your favorite food?" and "Does your favorite food require cooking?" Challenge students to add questions to their legends and provide ways to show this information. For instance, they might add directions to color the plate or add a pattern to the place mat.

Explore More

Math Conduct a probability test with students. Cut out and place all the pizza toppings (page 46) in a paper bag. If desired, add other toppings cut from colored paper. Write the name of each topping on chart paper, and record how many of each are in the bag. (You might use equal amounts or vary them.) Ask students to predict which topping will be pulled out of the bag most often in ten pulls. Then invite volunteers to take turns pulling a topping from the bag. On the chart, draw a tally mark beside each topping as it is pulled from the bag. (Make sure students return the topping to the bag after each turn.) After ten turns, have students count how many times each shape was pulled. How do the results compare to their predictions?

Language Arts, Math   Make a pizza with the class. (In advance, check with families about food allergies and dietary restrictions.) Bring in all the ingredients and tools needed to make the pizza (you might use a boxed pizza kit). Then help students read the recipe, measure and mix the ingredients, and bake the pizza. After the pizza cools, have students share their ideas about how it should be sliced so that everyone gets an equal portion. Challenge students to determine what fraction of the whole each student will receive.

Math, Art   Invite students to use craft materials to create their own pizzas on large paper circles. When finished, have them cut their pizzas into six or eight slices. Then, working with small groups, use the pizzas to teach about fractions. For example, you might give three students each a slice of pizza and then ask what fraction of the pizza these three students have. Or you might ask what fraction of the pizza is left.

 Literature Links

Eating the Alphabet:
Fruits & Vegetables From A to Z
by Lois Ehlert
(Harcourt Brace Jovanovich, 1989).
From apples to zucchini, creative collages in vibrant colors make readers' mouths water over the delicious, nutritious foods featured on each page.

The Little Red Hen (Makes a Pizza)
by Philemon Sturges
(Dutton Children's Books, 1999).
When Little Red Hen craves pizza, she picks up the supplies and invites her friends to help her make the pizza. Of course, her friends are unwilling to help—until it's time to eat!

The Princess and the Pizza
by Mary Jane Auch
(Holiday House, 2002).
Princess Pauline competes with other princesses to win the heart of Prince Drupert and his mother, Queen Zelda. Will she be able to clear the last hurdle—a cooking contest?

What Food Is This?
by Rosemarie Hausherr
(Scholastic, 1994).
Riddles about different foods pique readers' curiosity and provide information about healthy foods, eating habits, and meal preparation.

My Favorite Food

(1) Do you use a fork or spoon to eat your favorite food?

	yes	no
Shape of Pizza	triangular	rectangular

(2) How does your favorite food taste?

	sweet	salty	sour	another taste
Number of Onions	2	3	4	5

(3) When do you enjoy eating your favorite food?

	breakfast	lunch	dinner	another time
Number of Mushrooms	fewer than 3	more than 2 but fewer than 5	exactly 5	more than 5 but fewer than 8

(4) What is the texture of your favorite food?

	creamy	chewy	crunchy	another texture
Color of Place Mat	green	red	blue	orange

(5) Which food group does your favorite food belong to?

	fruits	vegetables	dairy	meats and beans	grains	other
Color of Napkin	gray	tan	pink	purple	yellow	white

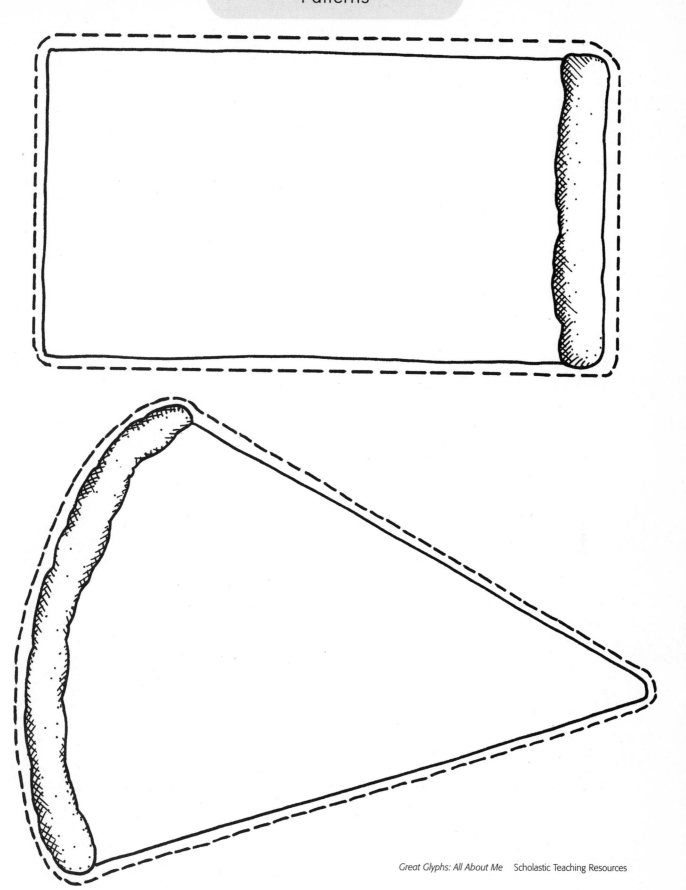

Great Glyphs: All About Me   Scholastic Teaching Resources

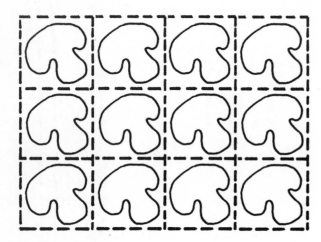

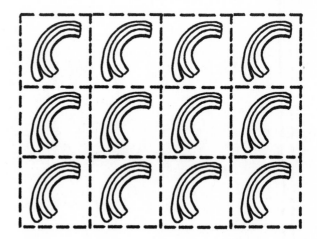

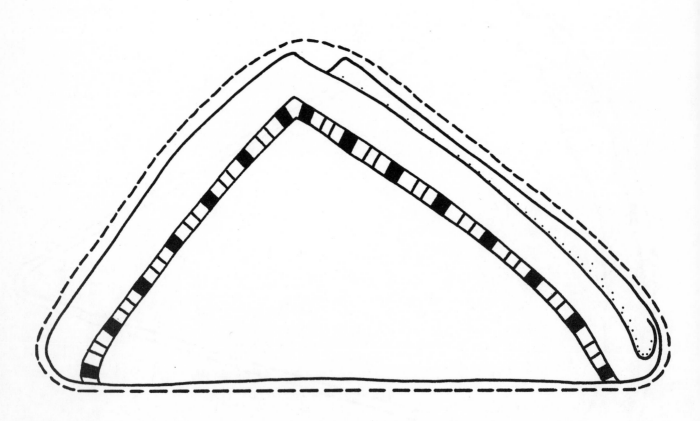

Time to Play

Square head: Favorite time to play is between 12:00 P.M. and 4:00 P.M.

Left-pointing eyes: Would rather play outdoors in October, November, or December

ABC/ABC pattern on body: Would rather do an outdoor activity that is different than choices listed

Blue robot: Would rather draw a picture on a rainy day

Math Skills

- geometry: shapes

- concepts of time: A.M./P.M. and months of year

- directionality: up, down, left, right

- patterns

Creating the Glyph

Distribute copies of the robot glyph patterns and the legend to students. Review the legend, one characteristic at a time, as you display a glyph you have already completed. Then distribute the other materials, and invite students to create their own personal robot glyph. Have students glue their glyph onto construction paper for a sturdy backing and draw antennae on the robot's head.

Critical Thinking

Display all the glyphs and play a game of Ten Questions. Have students take turns choosing a "secret glyph" and giving clues to classmates to help them identify which glyph they chose. Encourage students to analyze the data shown on the glyphs and include this information in their clues. For example, "The glyph I chose shows that the student would rather draw a picture on a rainy day" or "This glyph shows that the student would rather play soccer." After each clue is revealed, have the class eliminate the glyphs that do not fit the criteria until they have narrowed it down to one.

Materials

- reproducible glyph patterns and legend (pages 49–51)

- completed robot glyph

- 9- by12-inch construction paper

- scissors

- glue or paste

- crayons

Explore More

Math Reinforce learning about patterns. Provide students with a supply of small objects that they might use in their play activities, such as interlocking blocks, plastic coins, and shape manipulatives. Then invite students to use the objects to create two-, three-, and four-part patterns, such as AB/AB, ABC/ABC, ABB/ABB, ABAC/ABAC, and ABCD/ABCD. After exploring different ways to create patterns, have partners work together. Have one student start a pattern with the objects, and then have the other student continue the pattern.

Language Arts Play Guess the Toy with students. First, gather a collection of toys and put them in a large box. Tell students that you will secretly remove a toy from the box and then describe it to the class. Explain that you will keep the toy hidden as you give clues about its identity, but you will not use the name of the toy in your clues. When a student guesses the identity of the toy, remove it from its hiding place and show it to the class. Invite that student to pick a toy from the box, keeping it hidden, and then give clues about the toy until a classmate guesses its identity. Continue playing until every student has had a turn to describe a mystery toy. Alternatively, play a game of 20 Questions, with students asking questions to help them determine the identity of the toy.

Language Arts, Art Ask students to imagine they are robots. How would they look and act? Invite students to use an assortment of art materials to build the kind of robot that they'd like to be. When finished, have them write a story from the robot's perspective about an experience or adventure the robot might have. Create a bulletin board display with the stories and art projects.

Literature Links

Bicycle Book
by Gail Gibbons (Holiday House, 1995).
Colorful illustrations, informative facts, and simple explanations about bicycles—the history and science, types, and how to care for and safely ride them—keep readers engaged.

It's Great to Skate: An Easy Guide to In-line Skating
by Alexa Witt (Simon & Schuster Books for Young Readers, 2000).
Readers learn the basics of in-line skating with this humorous, easy-to-read book.

Rhinos Who Skateboard
by Julie Mammano
(Chronicle Books, 1999).
Fun-loving rhinos try different maneuvers and moves on their brightly decorated skateboards. This book includes a glossary of terms related to the exciting sport of skateboarding.

Time to Play

1 When is your favorite time to play?

	before 12:00 P.M.	between 12:00 P.M. and 4:00 P.M.	after 4:00 P.M.
Shape of Head	oval	square	circle

2 In which months would you rather play outdoors?

	January, February, or March	April, May, or June	July, August, or September	October, November, or December
Direction of Eyes				

3 What would you rather do indoors on a rainy day?

	play a board game	put together a puzzle	draw a picture	another activity
Color of Robot	orange	red	blue	green

4 What would you rather play outdoors? Use six shapes to make a pattern.

	play tag	play soccer	ride bikes	another activity
Pattern on Body	AB/AB pattern	AAB/AAB pattern	ABA/ABA pattern	ABC/ABC pattern

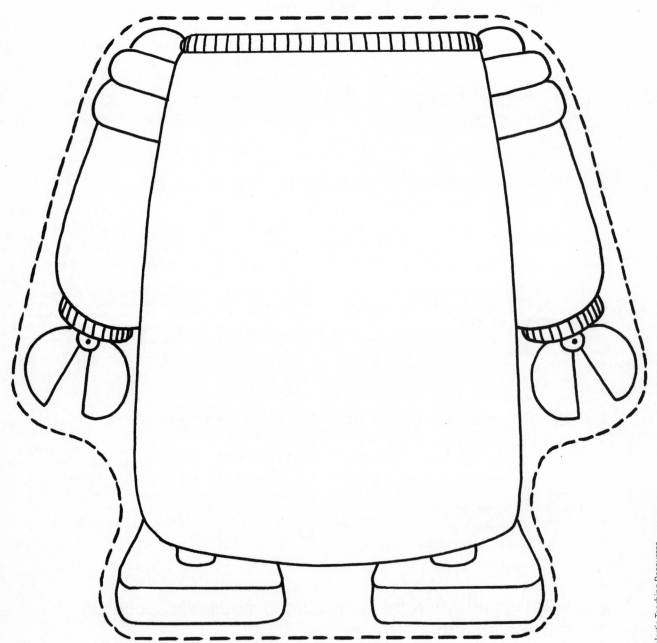

Great Glyphs: All About Me   Scholastic Teaching Resources

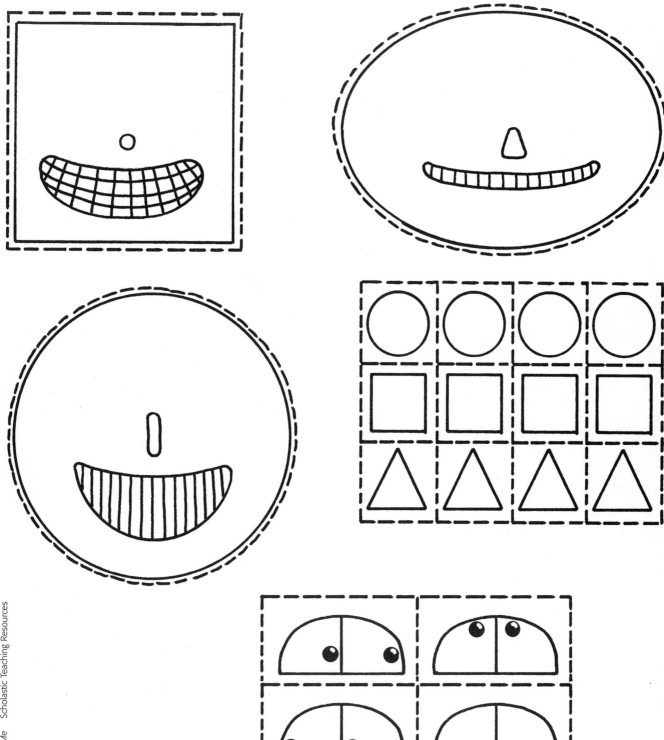

Sports Jersey

Two stripes on sleeves: Has played on a sports team

Red jersey: Favorite sport is played outdoors

Star: Favorite sport is played with a ball

Even number less than 50: Would rather play favorite sport in the fall

Creating the Glyph

1. Distribute copies of the jersey glyph patterns and legend to students. Review the legend, one characteristic at a time, as you display a glyph you have already completed. Then distribute the other materials, and invite students to create their own personal jersey glyph.

2. For question 4, have students write a two-digit number on the shape.

3. Have students glue their glyph onto construction paper for a sturdy backing. Invite them to draw a self-portrait wearing the jersey.

Critical Thinking

Ask students to predict whether or not more students' favorite sports require a ball. After students make their predictions, work with them to create a method that will help verify the question. One method students might use is to draw two large circles on the chalkboard, one labeled "Yes" and the other labeled "No." Have each student attach his or her glyph to the appropriate circle. Challenge students to count and compare the number of glyphs in each circle and then write the results in comparison sentences, using the signs for greater than, less than, and equal to. Have them use the comparison sentences to determine whether their predictions were correct. Encourage students to use the same method to predict and check other questions as well.

Explore More

Math, Movement   Students will "have a ball" taking part in different activities at a field day. Plan activities that involve the use of balls, such as shooting baskets, bouncing balls, or throwing and catching different sizes of balls. Ask students to work with partners to record their results for each event. At the end of the field day, have students write their results for each event on a chart.

Math   Have students write the name of three sports on a sheet of paper. Then invite them to poll 15 classmates to learn which of the three sports is their favorite. Instruct students to keep track of the responses by drawing a tally mark beside each sport that a classmate chooses. When finished, students can count their tally marks and then use the results to create a graph to share with the class.

Language Arts   Ask students to imagine that their new pen pal has never played their favorite sport. Have students write a letter to their pen pal to tell him or her how to play the sport, where it is played, what equipment is needed to play, and why they enjoy the sport. They might add illustrations and diagrams to enhance their explanations.

Literature Links

Play Ball, Amelia Bedelia
by Peggy Parish (Harper & Row, 1972).
This fun-filled tale features Amelia Bedelia as she fills in for a player on a baseball team.

Players in Pigtails
by Shana Corey (Scholastic Press, 2003).
In this delightful historical fiction story, readers learn interesting facts about the All-American Girls Professional Baseball League of the 1940s.

Take Me Out to the Ball Game
by Jack Norworth
(Four Winds Press, 1993).
Bold, colorful pictures that highlight the 1949 World Series between the Dodgers and Yankees accompany the words to this classic song.

Sports Jersey

1 Have you ever played on a sports team? Draw black stripes on the sleeves.

	yes	no
Number of Stripes on Each Sleeve	2	3

2 Where do you play your favorite sport?

	indoors	outdoors	both
Color of Jersey	yellow	red	blue

3 Is your favorite sport played with a ball?

	yes	no
Shape on Jersey	star	circle

4 In which season would you rather play your favorite sport? Write a two-digit number in the shape.

	fall	winter	spring	summer
Number in Shape	even number less than 50	odd number less than 50	even number greater than 50	odd number greater than 50

Weather Window

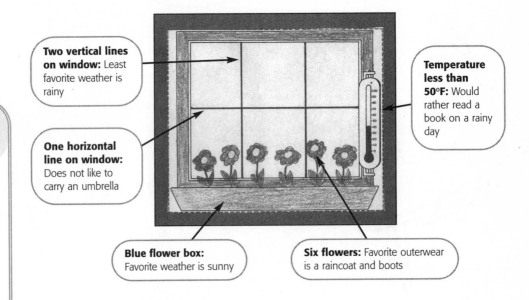

Two vertical lines on window: Least favorite weather is rainy

One horizontal line on window: Does not like to carry an umbrella

Temperature less than 50ºF: Would rather read a book on a rainy day

Blue flower box: Favorite weather is sunny

Six flowers: Favorite outerwear is a raincoat and boots

Math Skills

- geometry: horizontal and vertical lines
- counting
- one-to-one correspondence
- measurement: temperature
- greater than, less than, equal to

Materials

- reproducible glyph patterns and legend (pages 58–59)
- completed window glyph
- rulers
- scissors
- glue or paste
- crayons

Creating the Glyph

1. Distribute copies of the weather window glyph patterns and the legend to students. Review the legend, one characteristic at a time, as you display a glyph you have completed. Then distribute the other materials, and invite students to use the legend to create their own personal window glyph.

2. For questions 2 and 3, have students use rulers to draw horizontal or vertical lines in their window. Show them how to space the lines evenly so that the window is divided into equal-sized "panes."

Critical Thinking

Ask students to sequence the glyphs by the temperature shown on the thermometer. Then have them interpret data on specific glyphs. Ask questions, such as:

- *Which weather does the person with the highest temperature on his or her thermometer enjoy most?*
- *Which kind of outerwear does the person with a temperature of 50ºF on his or her thermometer like best?*
- *Do two or more glyphs show the same temperature on the thermometer? What other features do they have in common? What do the features mean?*

Explore More

Math   Place a thermometer outside a window so that students can easily see it from within the classroom. Each day for two weeks, have students read and record the outdoor temperature. At the end of the two weeks, invite them to use their findings in a variety of math activities. For example, you might have them find what the temperature difference was from one day to the next during that time period. Or they might graph their results to create a visual representation of how the temperature changed during the recording period.

Science, Language Arts   Designate a specific window in your classroom or another area of your school as the Weather Window. Have children visit the window daily to observe and record the outdoor weather conditions for that day. (If the weather changes during the day, you might invite students to return to the window to observe the changes.) At the end of each day, ask students to write a summary of the weather in their journals, including how it might have affected their choices of activities and clothing.

Language Arts   As a follow-up to observing the weather in the above activity, invite students to write poems about different kinds of weather. There are lots of great examples of weather poetry to share with children. Share a few examples for inspiration, such as poems from *Sky Words*, by Marilyn Singer (Maxwell Macmillan International, 1994), or *Weather*, by Lee Bennett Hopkins (HarperCollins, 1994). Then invite students to choose a type of weather and write a poem about it.

 Literature Links

Feel the Wind
by Arthur Dorros (Crowell, 1989).
Simple text and playful illustrations explain what causes the wind, how it helps us, and how it affects our weather and environment. The author includes instructions on how to make a weather vane.

Flash, Crash, Rumble, and Roll
by Franklyn M. Branley (Crowell, 1964).
This book uses appealing illustrations and diagrams to explore the causes of the thunder and lightning that come with thunderstorms.

Weather Words and What They Mean
by Gail Gibbons (Holiday House, 1990).
Attractive illustrations and clear explanations of basic weather terms and concepts help readers learn about topics such as temperature, air pressure, moisture, and wind.

What Will the Weather Be?
by Lynda DeWitt (HarperCollins, 1991).
This book introduces basic weather characteristics, instruments, and vocabulary, as well how meteorologists gather information for their forecasts.

Weather Window

1 Which kind of weather do you most enjoy?

	cloudy	sunny	snowy	another kind
Color of Flower Box	green	blue	red	yellow

2 Which kind of weather do you like the least? Draw lines from top to bottom.

	windy	rainy	icy	another kind
Number of Vertical Lines on Window	1	2	3	4

3 Do you like to carry an umbrella? Draw lines from side to side.

	no	yes
Number of Horizontal Lines on Window	1	2

4 Which would you rather do on a rainy day? Color in the thermometer.

	read a book	do a puzzle	play a game
Temperature on Thermometer	less than 50ºF	exactly 50ºF	greater than 50ºF

5 Which kind of outerwear do you like best? Draw flowers.

	sunglasses and sun hat	raincoat and boots	jacket and cap
Number of Flowers in Flower Box	4	6	8

A Sunny Future for Me

Wavy rays: Does not know what he or she wants to be when grows up

ABB/ABB pattern on rays: Would like to live in another state

Eyes pointing up: Would like to have a different job than choices listed

Red center: Would like to live in a large or small city

Math Skills

• patterns

• directionality: left, right, up, down

Materials

• reproducible glyph patterns and legend (pages 62–64)

• completed sun glyph

• scissors

• glue or paste

• crayons

Creating the Glyph

Distribute copies of the sun glyph patterns and the legend to students. Review the legend, one characteristic at a time, as you display a glyph you have already completed. Then distribute the other materials, and invite students to create their own personal sun glyph.

Critical Thinking

Ask students to guess which kind of job—making or selling things, helping people or animals, entertaining people, or another job—most students would rather have when they grow up. Then ask students to tell how they could use their completed sun glyphs to find the actual answer. Once they share their ideas, suggest that they place their glyphs in four groups according to the direction of the eyes on the sun. Then have students count the glyphs in each group to find out which type of job most would prefer. Repeat for other questions on the glyph.

Explore More

Math Display students' glyphs in groups according to where they would rather live when they grow up. Have students count the number of glyphs in each group, write that number on a sticky note, and attach the number near the group of glyphs. Then ask students to count the total number of glyphs. Have them use the numbers to express part-to-whole relationships. For example, they might state that 7 out of 25 students would rather live in another state when they grow up. Repeat the activity with other information.

Social Studies   Play charades with the class. Invite students to take turns acting out the kind of job they would like to do when they grow up. Give the class ten tries to guess what job each student is portraying. Ask students to tell why they are interested in particular jobs.

Social Studies, Language Arts   Write the names of different jobs on separate index cards. Then collect pictures of tools or play tools related to the kinds of jobs printed on the cards. Try to include at least three tools that can be used for each job. Place all the tools on a table. Then divide the class into small groups and give each group a card. Have the students in each group read the job named on their card and then work together to gather the tools that are used in that job. When finished, ask each group to show each tool in its collection to the class and tell why that tool was chosen.

Language Arts, Social Studies   Ask students if they know what they would like to be when they grow up. For those who do, invite them to write out a plan that shows how they might accomplish that goal. In their plans they might include steps such as making good grades, graduating, learning how to use a computer, learning other special skills, and so on. Invite those students who are not sure about what they want to be when they grow up to write about the kinds of things they enjoy doing or are good at doing. Then encourage them to explore a variety of books about careers to see if they can match some of their interests and abilities to a specific career.

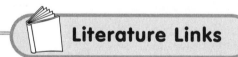

Literature Links

Community Helpers From A to Z
by Bobbie Kalman (Niki Walker Crabtree Publishing Company, 1998).
This alphabetical collection of community helpers features photographs of people and the important jobs they do.

Jobs People Do
by Christopher Maynard (DK Publishing, 1997).
Children dressed up as lawyers, mail carriers, pilots, ballet dancers, chefs, and more help young readers explore 50 different occupations.

When You Grow Up
by Lennie Goodings
(Phyllis Fogelman Books, 2001).
A bear encourages her young son to consider the many career possibilities he might choose from, such as being a pilot, a soccer star, or even a sheriff.

A Sunny Future for Me

1 Do you know what you want to be when you grow up?

	yes	no
Shape of Sun		

2 Where would you rather live when you grow up? Color the rays to make a pattern.

	in the town or city I live in now	in another town or city, but in the same state	in another state	in another country
Pattern on Sun Rays	AB/AB	ABC/ABC	ABB/ABB	ABA/ABA

3 What kind of place would you want to live in when you grow up?

	in a large or small city	in a suburb	in the country	in another place
Color of Center of Sun	red	orange	yellow	pink

4 Which kind of job would you rather have when you grow up?

	making or selling things	helping people or animals	entertaining people	another job
Direction of Eyes				

Great Glyphs: All About Me   Scholastic Teaching Resources